Bibliographical Series
of Supplements to 'British Book News'
on Writers and Their Work

★

GENERAL EDITOR
Bonamy Dobrée

HORACE WALPOLE
from a portrait of 1754 by J. G. ECCARDT *in
the National Portrait Gallery.*

HORACE WALPOLE

by

HUGH HONOUR

'*I have Conway-papers to sort; I have Lives of the Painters to write; I have my prints to paste, my house to build, and everything in the world to tell posterity.—How am I to find time for all this?*'—Horace Walpole to H. S. Conway, 28 June 1760.

PUBLISHED FOR

THE BRITISH COUNCIL
and the NATIONAL BOOK LEAGUE

BY LONGMANS, GREEN & CO., LONDON, NEW YORK, TORONTO

LONGMANS, GREEN & CO. LTD.
6 & 7 Clifford Street, London W.1
Thibault House, Thibault Square, Cape Town
605–611 Lonsdale Street, Melbourne, C.1

LONGMANS, GREEN & CO. INC.
55 Fifth Avenue, New York 3

LONGMANS, GREEN & CO.
20 Cranfield Road, Toronto 16

ORIENT LONGMANS PRIVATE LTD.
Calcutta   Bombay   Madras
Delhi   Hyderabad   Dacca

First published in 1957

© *Hugh Honour 1957*

Printed in Great Britain at The Curwen Press, Plaistow, E.13

CONTENTS

¶ Horatio Walpole, the son of Sir Robert Walpole, was born on 24 September 1717. He succeeded his nephew as fourth Earl of Orford in 1791 and died on 2 March 1797.

HORACE WALPOLE

I

ARIEL THE SPRITE IN A SPLIT SHOE

When the Rev. Mr. Seward visited the Earl of Hertford at Ragley Park in 1758 he was greatly astonished at the antics of a fellow guest, who described the encounter in a letter to a friend:

> Strolling about the house, he saw me first sitting on the pavement of the lumber room with Louis, all over cobwebs and dirt and mortar; then found me in his own room on a ladder writing on a picture: and half an hour afterwards lying on the grass in the court with the dogs and the children, in my slippers and without my hat. He had some doubt whether I was the painter or the factotum of the family; but you would have died at his surprise when he saw me walk into dinner dressed and sit by Lady Hertford. Lord Lyttelton was there, and the conversation turned on literature: finding me not quite ignorant added to the parson's wonder; but he could not contain himself any longer, when after dinner he saw me go to romps and jumping with the two boys; he broke out to my Lady Hertford, and begged to know who and what sort of a man I really was, for he had never met with anything of the kind.

It is wholly characteristic of Horace Walpole that this most vivid of his self-portraits should, so far from being introspective, be seen entirely through the startled eyes of a spectator. Such rare glimpses as he allows us of himself are all from the outside: and if we try to catch him unaware and off his guard he vanishes, giving us the slip like Proteus, or like 'Ariel the sprite in a split shoe' as he once described himself when earth-bound by gout. We may stalk him through the routs, the masquerades and ridottos of eighteenth-century London, we may follow him in and out of the salons of Paris or along the serpentine avenues of English landscaped parks and around his favourite crumbling 'follies',[1] thick

[1] The eighteenth-century landscape garden was usually decorated with a variety of small buildings—temples, summer-houses and ruins—which may by classified as 'follies'. Artificial ruins enjoyed popularity both for their picturesque qualities and the melancholy sensations they aroused in spectators.

with the 'true rust of the Barons' wars', until at last we may fancy to have cornered him in the vaulted gallery of his neat Gothic castle at Strawberry Hill, but even here he eludes us and we are left, as always, clutching a mask.

Man of the world or valetudinarian recluse, patient scholar or idling dilettante, 'dancing senator' or active backstairs politician; these are only some of the many roles which Horace Walpole could assume at will to amuse or edify his varied acquaintance and also, perhaps, to shield his tender susceptibilities from the public gaze. Although he has left some 4,000 letters, he seems to have defied us almost wilfully to apprehend his true character, so that nearly every generalization about him, no matter how firmly based on one of his own remarks, can be modified if not contradicted in the light of another statement. Nor did his contemporaries, even those who knew him well, find him any easier to comprehend. They can tell of his appearance, his simple elegance of attire, his slim boyish figure and his bright, penetrating, lively dark eyes. They describe his gait on entering a room, '*chapeau bras* between his hands as if he wished to compress it, or under his arm—knees bent, and feet on tiptoe, as if afraid of a wet floor', and how he would 'scatter his wit and *petit mots* with dazzling profusion' to entertain a circle of bluestockings. But even that virtuoso of literary portraiture, James Boswell, could manage nothing better than a bald reference to 'Horry's constitutional tranquility or affectation of it.' And Gilly Williams who had known him since boyhood, adds little with his facile comment, 'I can figure no being happier than Horry. *Mostrari digito praetereuntium* has been his whole aim. For this he has wrote, printed and built.' No doubt Walpole felt the spur of fame, but as for happiness, it was only another mask. 'I love to communicate my satisfactions,' he wrote, but added rather wistfully, 'my melancholy I generally shut up in my own breast.'

Born in 1717, Horace Walpole was the youngest son of Sir Robert Walpole, the great Whig First Minister and virtual dictator of England from 1721 to 1742, when he fell from office and was elevated to the peerage as first Earl of Orford. The Walpoles belonged to the squirearchy rather than to the ancient aristocracy, but Sir Robert's great wealth and political power enabled Horace to enjoy the education of a typical English milord of the period—Eton, King's College, Cambridge, and then the Grand Tour when he idled away two years in Italy with his school-fellow Thomas Gray the poet. Already, before leaving the University, he had been fortified with the first of the sinecures which permitted him, on his return to England, to continue indefinitely a gentlemanly life of leisure, oscillating between a handsome London house and a summer retreat at Strawberry Hill, with frequent rounds of country house visits and an occasional trip to Paris. In this genial fashion he sauntered through life, untroubled by material wants or cares; and nothing gross or mean was ever allowed to disrupt the exquisite harmony he had created for himself—not even his accession to the Earldom of Orford in 1791, when he became 'the poorest peer in England'. He died in 1797 at the age of 79, by then a lonely survivor in the era of the French Revolution and *Lyrical Ballads*, from a remote world of periwigs, Jacobite conspiracies and the polished couplets of Pope.

One may see in such a life an epitome of all the blessings of the eighteenth century, and Walpole would have warmly agreed with Talleyrand that only those who had lived before the Revolution knew *la douceur de vivre*. Antiquary, novelist, poetaster, social charmer, architect, gardener and political chronicler; all these diverse parts could be cultivated and enjoyed together in civilized harmony by one so fortunately placed as Horace Walpole—albeit he was unique in having both the opportunity and the talents. No other figure of his time combined an equal variety of gifts; and his character, so intangible yet so beguiling, lures us on to read every scrap he wrote, and to consider each of the interests which form the background to his life's work.

II

THE ANTIQUARY

As an antiquary Horace Walpole must be regarded primarily as a gentleman amateur, and he was indeed an exceptionally well marked specimen of this peculiarly English species. In no other country have amateurs played so large a part in the arts and sciences. The names of Lord Bacon, Sir Thomas Browne, Sir John Suckling, the Earl of Rochester, Thomas Gray, William Beckford and Jane Austen, will suffice to indicate the extent of their contribution to literature. In the visual arts, Lord Burlington set the canons of architectural taste for half a century, and Dr. Thomas Monro schooled a generation of water-colour painters (including Turner and Girtin), while physicists and naturalists still owe a debt to the Hon. Robert Boyle and the Rev. Gilbert White.

The amateur antiquaries of the seventeenth and early eighteenth centuries had few though formidable professional rivals, and much valuable research was carried out by retiring clerics, lawyers and doctors, who spent their leisure hours in delving into the history of their local monuments. Eccentric characters such as William Somner of Canterbury, Elizabeth Elstob—the 'Saxon nymph'—Ralph Thoresby of Leeds and William Stukeley—the arch-druid—have an honoured place in the history of English archaeology. To this admirable tradition Horace Walpole was proud to belong and his loyalty to it is one of his most endearing qualities. When professionals and would-be professionals trounced him for his amateurishness he became all the more jealous of his amateur status. 'Pray, my dear child, don't compliment me any more upon my learning; there is nobody so superficial', he protested to Horace Mann,

> Except a little history, a little poetry, a little painting and some divinity, I know nothing. How should I? I, who have always lived

in the big busy world; who lie abed all the morning calling it morning as long as you please; who sup in company; who have played at pharaoh half my life, and now at loo till two or three in the morning; who have always loved pleasure; haunted auctions—in short, who don't know as much astronomy as would carry me to Knightsbridge, nor more physic than a physician, nor in short anything that is called science. If it were not that I lay up a little provision in summer, like the ant, I should be as ignorant as all the people I live with.

These words, which excited the spleen of Macaulay, echo an anti-professional theme which runs through English literature in the eighteenth century and are a clear exposition of the amateur's point of view. Moreover, they reflect Walpole's gentlemanly affectation of an indolence he did not in fact possess, for he worked at his historical pieces as assiduously as the most professional dryasdust. His inaccuracies, and they are many and serious, arose from a weakness for jumping to conclusions and not from any want of application. But these errors which so shocked the contemporary pedants now stand out no more than the mistakes of the pedants themselves, while Walpole's works are distinguished by an elegance of expression and lightness of touch which theirs all too conspicuously lack.

Walpole made his debut as an antiquary in 1758, when he published his *Catalogue of Royal and Noble Authors*, printed in a limited edition at his private press.[1] The two slender volumes contain accounts of the lives and writings of members of the English Royal Family and nobility from Richard I to Frederick Prince of Wales who had died in 1751. Although the catalogue is by no means complete and was, as Walpole insisted, 'calculated for the closets of the *idle* and *inquisitive*', it contains much curious information culled from obscure

[1] Horace Walpole initiated his private printing press at Strawberry Hill in 1757. This press enabled him to print small editions of his works for circulation among his friends, *vers de societé* with which to welcome lady visitors to the house, title pages and bookplates. He used it also for reprinting scarce books and for the publication of a few modern works of which Gray's *Odes* is by far the most notable.

sources, and may still be read with pleasure for its droll anecdotes, ingenious conjectures and brilliant thumb-nail portraits. Nevertheless one must, in this instance, agree with the dyspeptic Macaulay that Walpole rejected, with too gay an abandon, whatever appeared dull while retaining only 'what is in itself amusing or can be made so by the artifice of his diction'.

Much as it pleased the polite society for which it was intended, the *Catalogue of Royal and Noble Authors* met with little but scorn from professional scholars and single-minded bibliophiles who were quick to belabour its author for omissions and inaccuracies. Undeterred by their captious criticisms, Walpole set about a more grandiose project—the first comprehensive history of English art. Having acquired the manuscript note-books in which George Vertue, the engraver, had jotted down every tittle he heard, read or saw concerning English art, he scoured the little volumes to compile his *Anecdotes of Painting in England*, adding pertinent reflections of his own. The informative value of the completed work was due to Vertue's assiduity, as he readily acknowledged; but Walpole must be credited with having extracted a readable and entertaining book from an unwieldy tangle of manuscript notes. Nor was it without persistent labour over a number of years, aided by convenient fits of gout, that he achieved this end. For nearly two centuries, *The Anecdotes of Painting* has been the essential source, the Vasari's *Lives* so to speak, for the study of English art, and even today it has not entirely been superseded by the publication in full of the manuscripts on which it was based.

In the preface to the first volume of the *Anecdotes*, Walpole prophesied that the age which had just opened with the accession of George III would be the most fruitful in the history of English art. But when, twenty years later, he added a brief survey of the period in which this prediction had been so abundantly fulfilled he dwelt little on the portraits of Reynolds and Gainsborough, and did not so much as mention the landscapes of Richard Wilson or the animal paintings of Stubbs. His encomiums were reserved for the miniatures of Lady Lucan who 'transferred the vigour of Raphael to her copies in water-colour', the drawings of Lady Diana Beauclerk whose figures were 'equal to what a Grecian statuary would have formed', and Mrs. Damer's busts which were 'not inferior to the antique'. No one was better equipped than Walpole to appreciate the leading artists of his day and, as his correspondence testifies, no one wrote more judicious appraisals of them; but there is a provoking element of caprice in all his criticism of contemporary arts and letters. Happily, the volume which opens with these courtly but irrelevant eulogies closes with an essay on landscape gardening which is at once the best account of its subject and Walpole's most exquisite piece of formal prose—if one may describe as formal a prose style so closely resembling the artful informality of an eighteenth-century park.

A landscape gardener himself in a small way, and a tireless visitor to country estates, both 'improved' and undergoing 'improvement', he was uniquely qualified to write of this most typically English of all the arts, and his letters no less than his essay reveal a discriminating eye for its true excellence. This passion also discloses an aspect of his character. The bleak and uncouth wilds of the Lake District held no charms for Walpole as they did for his friend Gray; for him nature was always bounded by the belt of trees that surrounds the park, and his youthful cry of exultation near the Grand Chartreuse—'Precipices, mountains, torrents, wolves, rumblings, Salvator Rosa'—springs from the amateur of paintings rather than the romantic. Nothing shows Walpole's allegiance to his times more clearly than his attitude to nature which he preferred when tamed and improved, though not entirely subdued by art—like manners, his own natural style of writing and even, perhaps, history.

Whilst dallying with the *Anecdotes of Painting*, Walpole completed a piece of research of less certain value: *Historic*

Doubts on the Reign of King Richard III, the first of a weari-
somely long and still continuing line of valiant attempts to
exculpate that unhappy monarch. The mistaken interpreta-
tion of a crucial document invalidates Walpole's thesis and
its shrill argumentative tone makes it the least attractive of
his productions. But the slender volume throws another
beam of light on his character, for his defence of Richard III
is conducted with the passionate ardour of a personal
feud. Deeply read in all the medieval literature available to
him, Walpole came to regard historical figures as his inti-
mate friends, so that when the *Paston Letters* were first published in 1787 he plunged delightedly into them, remarking
to Lady Ossory:

> There are letters from *all* my acquaintance, Lord Rivers, Lord
> Hastings, the Earl of Warwick, whom I remember still better than
> Mrs. Strawbridge though she died within these fifty years. What
> antiquary would be answering a letter from a living Countess, when
> he may read one from Eleanor Mowbray, Duchess of Norfolk.

The past afforded him a pleasant escape, and his vision of it
is not unclouded by sensibility. 'Old castles, old pictures, old
histories and the babble of old people make one live back
into the centuries that cannot disappoint one', he wrote.
'One holds fast and surely what is past. The dead have
exhausted their power of deceiving; one can trust Catherine
of Medicis now.'

III

THE SQUIRE OF STRAWBERRY HILL

Walpole's attitude to the past, and indeed to life itself,
found its most notable and characteristic expression in his
villa at Strawberry Hill. In 1747 he rented 'a little plaything
house' by the Thames at Twickenham, so small, he told
Sir Horace Mann, 'that I can send it you in a letter to look
at: the prospect is as delightful as possible, commanding the
river, the town, and Richmond Park; and being situated on

a hill descends to the Thames through two or three little meadows, where I have some Turkish sheep and cows, all studied in their colours for becoming the view'. He bought the house in 1749 and spent the next forty years transforming it into the miniature gothic castle with which his name will always be associated. A devout admirer of Palladian architecture, he considered the classical style proper only for magnificent and public buildings since 'columns and all their beautiful ornaments look ridiculous when crowded into a closet or a cheese-cake house', and he therefore resolved on the 'charming and venerable gothic' for his Sabine farm.

The 'Modern Gothick' which a builders' compendium of 1736 declared to be 'known for its disposition, and by its affected Lightness, Delicacy, and over-rich, even whimsical Decoration' was well established as a suitable decorative style for garden pavilions or occasional rooms before 1750. As Sir Kenneth Clark has remarked, Strawberry Hill was 'no original venture, but the chief example of a prevalent fashion'. Nevertheless, it was not entirely without originality and its place in the history of a movement which spread across Europe in the late eighteenth century and changed the face of England's towns in the nineteenth, must not be under-estimated.

The historical importance of Strawberry Hill—and of several of Horace Walpole's literary works—rests mainly upon the social prestige of their author, who stamped with the seal of fashionable approbation a style which had been regarded hitherto as a pleasing whimsicality comparable with *chinoiserie*. But gothic had a very deep-rooted appeal for the English since it could be, and often was, regarded as pre-eminently the national style. Indeed, the success of the gothic revival was due largely to its potency in expressing the growing spirit of nationalism. As Mr. Wilmarth Lewis has pointed out, it represented a 'phase of national self-consciousness similar to that of America in 1920; when we built houses and public buildings in the colonial style'.

Strawberry Hill differs from all its predecessors and most of its contemporaries in two important ways—in the irregularity of its plan and in the archaeological accuracy of its detail. Enamoured of the 'Sharawaggi or Chinese want of symmetry in buildings as in grounds or gardens', Walpole abandoned the current practice of imposing fanciful gothic details on a rigid classical framework; and Strawberry is probably the first intentionally asymmetrical house built in England. Too ardent an antiquary to condone the meaningless rococo-gothic ornaments of the builders' repository, he based every detail on some medieval precedent, though with scant respect for the purpose of the original—a rose window in Old St. Paul's provided the model for a ceiling, the Chapter-house of York Minster was reduced to the proportions of a closet, and an archiepiscopal tomb did duty for a chimney-piece. But in the transformation each element was made lighter and more elegant to accord with Walpole's belief that gothic architecture and sculpture, like the natural landscape, might well be improved by the hand of Taste. However gothic they might claim to be, Horace Walpole and the committee of friends who helped to design Strawberry founded their concept of taste on the classical ideals of balance, nice proportions and good manners. Nor was their attitude far removed from that of contemporary neo-classical architects like the Adam brothers who had abandoned Palladio and were pillaging Roman antiquities for graceful details and decorative motifs to enrich their buildings. At Strawberry Hill, the surprisingly successful combination of romantic and classical values made the exterior as 'riant' as Walpole wished, and the interior less gloomy and monkish than he liked to think. Beside the uninhibited romantic *panache* of William Beckford's Fonthill Abbey, which was begun a year before Walpole died, Strawberry Hill seems a model of eighteenth-century propriety, reticence and decorum.

As the turrets and battlements of Strawberry rose, as its chambers were prettified by gay heraldic decorations and filled with a jackdaw's hoard of bric-à-brac, the house grew into one of the most attractive and one of the most famous in the kingdom. Set in 'enamelled meadows with filigree hedges' the exterior, machicolated, crocketed and pinnacled, was dominated by a great round tower. Inside there was a sombre hall dimly lit by 'lean windows fattened with rich saints', from which a staircase with 'the lightest gothic balustrade' led to a library whose bookcases were modelled on a screen in Old St. Paul's, a fan-vaulted gallery and numerous rooms hung with rich dark wall-papers. Walpole's original ideas for his summer retreat had been modest but they soon expanded, and from 1750 onwards a gently rippling Strawberry theme runs as a *leitmotif* through his letters which tell of the seasonable pursuits in the model park, of projected additions to the house, of new acquisitions to the collection and of the visitors who came from far and wide to inspect the raree-show. For the benefit of these visitors and the servants who showed them round, Walpole printed at his private press a *Description of Strawberry Hill* in which he meticulously catalogued every detail of decoration, every picture, every *objet d'art*, every relic of the great and every trifle of pottery with which he had so lovingly adorned it. 'Well', a gushing gentlewoman remarked to the exhausted cicerone, 'I must live another *forty* years to have time to see all the curiosities of this house.'

IV

A HEAD FILLED WITH GOTHIC STORY

Behind the painted windows and beneath the papier mâché fretted vault of his beloved Strawberry, Horace Walpole plunged ever more deeply into a medieval world of his own creation. Then, one June night in 1764 he had a dream of which he could only remember,

—that I thought myself in an ancient castle (a very natural dream for a head filled like mine with Gothic story), and that on the upper banister of the staircase I saw a gigantic hand in armour. In the evening I sat down to write without knowing for the very least what I intended to say or relate.

For two months he lived in a gothic phantasmagoria from which he emerged at last with *The Castle of Otranto*. He lost no time in publishing this *conte*, stating that it had been translated from an Italian black-letter original by William Marshal, Gent., but so immediate and widespread was its success that Walpole was not ashamed to acknowledge his authorship in the second edition which was soon demanded.

The scene of this gothic tale is set in a vast and gloomy castle in Southern Italy which, as might be expected, bears a strong resemblance to Strawberry Hill.[1] Its story is a confection of all the romantic elements—a wicked and lustful prince, his pious and long-suffering wife, a beautiful princess from a distant part of Italy, and her father who returns from the Holy Land to rescue her. The hero is, naturally, a young peasant of handsome appearance and true nobility of character who is eventually discovered, by a birth-mark, to be the rightful prince and marries the fair princess. Supernatural portents abound and Walpole wisely placed the grossest at the very beginning, after which the reader is prepared for anything that may follow, soon becoming as 'hardened to preternatural appearances' as the wicked Prince Manfred himself. Yet he may gasp, with amusement if not with horror, at the climax:

'Thou art no lawful prince', said Jerome; 'thou art no prince—Go discuss thy claim with Frederic; and when that is done—' 'It is done', replied Manfred; 'Frederic accepts Matilda's hand and is content to wave his claim, unless I have no male issue'.—As he

[1] The castle also has elements derived from Trinity College, Cambridge, as Walpole realized when he went there again some years after writing his novel. He also found, to his delight, that it was in some respects similar to the medieval castle at Otranto in Apulia.

spoke those words three drops of blood fell from the nose of Alfonso's statue. Manfred turned pale and the Princess sunk to her knees.

Dark and gothic as their surroundings are, the inhabitants of Otranto think and talk very much like the people of Horace Walpole's London, though they occasionally spice their conversation with a little tushery to give period flavour. The servants have stepped momentarily out of a Sheridan comedy (though Walpole thought they were Shakespearian) and the young ladies have drifted languidly upon this dismal scene from Richardson's polite society.

> 'Ah! Matilda, your heart is in danger—but let me warn you as a friend—he has owned to me that he is in love: it cannot be with you for yesterday was the first time you ever met—was it not?' 'Certainly' replied Matilda, 'But why does my dearest Isabella conclude from anything that I have said, that'—She paused—then continuing: 'He saw you first and I am far from having the vanity to think that my little portion of charms could engage a heart devoted to you. May you be happy Isabella, whatever is the fate of Matilda!'

Nor does the story lack those moments for tears occasioned by all the novels of the fashionable Sensibility cult, and one is scarcely surprised to learn, on the last page, that the hero 'was persuaded that he could know no happiness but in the society of one with whom he could for ever indulge the melancholy that had taken possession of his soul.'

A judicious mixture of tearful scenes and gothic horrors, which made some of Thomas Gray's friends at Cambridge 'cry a little, and all in general afraid to go to bed', secured for *The Castle of Otranto* an immediate success which was further increased when the identity of the author was discovered. Enthusiastically praised, dramatized and widely imitated, it fathered a monstrous progeny of Gothic novels including *The Castle of Wolfenbach, The Orphan of the Rhine, The Necromancer of the Black Forest* and *The Mysteries of Udolpho*, which are preserved in the spirit of Jane Austen's

satire. 'Are they all horrid,' asks Catherine Morland in
Northanger Abbey, 'are you sure they are all horrid?' Now
that the achievements of more sophisticated practitioners of
the supernatural—Edgar Allan Poe, Sheridan Le Fanu and
Montague James—have made these gothic romances appear
tame and often comic, it is a little difficult to understand the
wide and steady appeal which they held over the whole
reading public for some forty years. Still more difficult is it
to appreciate the profound impression such novels made,
not only on susceptible young ladies like Catherine Morland, but also on Byron, Keats and Coleridge all of whom
derived inspiration from them.

The importance of *The Castle of Otranto* is not, however, confined to its influence on tales of horror. By adapting
the conventions of the sensibility novel (of which Richardson's *Clarissa*, Sterne's *Sentimental Journey* and Goldsmith's
Vicar of Wakefield are the most notable and Henry Macken-
zie's *Man of Feeling* the most lachrymose examples) to a wild
and romantic tale set in a distant age, Walpole freed the
novel from the bounds of the contemporary scene and
opened a door to the historical imagination. However ridiculous its plot, however stilted its dialogue, however pre-
posterous its supernatural machinery, *The Castle of Otranto*
was, none the less, the first essay in that historical genre
which was to be so brilliantly developed by Sir Walter Scott
and his successors in the nineteenth century. It is therefore
an important literary phenomenon though, to the modern
reader, who is unwilling to be chilled into a pleasing horror
and unable to summon the tear of sensibility, it may appear
little more than a charmingly wayward late Georgian period
piece.

The gothic atmosphere of Strawberry Hill inspired
Walpole to write but one other imaginative work, *The
Mysterious Mother*, a tragedy whose theme and style are
adequately summarized in one agonized line—'Incest! Good
Heavens!' Confessedly 'horrid not polite', it is a distasteful
little piece in laboriously composed pseudo-Jacobean blank

verse that seldom sinks to the ridiculous and never rises to the sublime. Although one can but agree with Byron when he states that it is 'no puling love play', few will now support his assertion that it is 'of the highest order . . . the last tragedy in our language'. *The Mysterious Mother* contrasts strangely with Horace Walpole's other poetic works; pastoral love songs, nicely turned compliments to lady visitors, charades and epitaphs on bull-finches.

Were he to be judged solely by the works he published in his life time, Horace Walpole would occupy but a tiny gothic niche in the history of English literature. Always readable, usually interesting, never dull and invariably written in a limpid conversational prose, his published works are those of a gentleman who dabbled in literature. To compare his historical writing with that of Gibbon, his novel with that of Goldsmith or his verses with those of Gray would be merely invidious. Nevertheless, it is as difficult to be level-headed about Walpole's literary as his architectural fantasies, for they form part also of his greatest work, his correspondence, where they appear transmuted by the glow of his personality. *The Anecdotes of Painting* and *The Castle of Otranto* are books within a greater book, and devotees of Horace Walpole come to look on them with the affectionate respect Proustians might accord to Swann's essay on Jan Vermeer of Delft. Whereas the letters of many writers—Shelley or Keats for example—are read principally to illuminate their author's published works, Walpole's published works are valued principally for the light they throw on his letters. And it is idle to speculate on what his literary position would have been if his letters had not survived, for he took every care that these apparently most ephemeral of his writings should be preserved.

V

THE LETTER WRITER

If Walpole's approach to the works he intended for immediate publication seems a little amateurish, the way in which
he managed his correspondence betrays a markedly different
attitude. Naturally communicative about everything except
his inner self, he felt a vocation to record whatever interested
him or might amuse his friends. This obsession found an
outlet in a projected history of his own times to be modelled,
perhaps, on that of his favourite Bishop Burnet, with whom
he shared the gift of portraying people as if he had come
straight from their bed-chambers. A start was made on this
ambitious work and a mass of material (including a collection of all contemporary plays and pamphlets) was assembled,
when it occurred to him, with a flash of original and remarkable insight, that his private correspondence was a more
convenient and, because of its immediacy and flexibility, a
much more suitable vehicle for the purpose he designed.
'Nothing gives so just an idea of an age as genuine letters,'
he wrote, 'nay, history waits for its seal from them.' He
was consequently forced to be business-like about the choice
of ostensible recipients for letters that were in fact intended
for posterity. To each of his friends he wrote from a slightly
different view-point, and when a correspondence was in-
terrupted by death or estrangement he had, perforce, to find
a suitable successor. To George Montagu, for example, he
wrote about the gossip of the town for some thirty years,
and when he quarrelled with him, continued the story without a break in letters to the Countess of Upper Ossory.
Thomas Gray was the recipient of letters on antiquities and
the arts which, after his death, were sent to his biographer,
the Rev. William Mason. Fortunately, however, the essential
strand in the fabric of Walpole's vast correspondence was not
broken in forty-five years, for Sir Horace Mann, the British
Envoy in Florence whom he had met on the grand tour,

remained his friend from 1740 to 1785, though they never saw each other again. By writing regularly to Mann he was able to draw the main outlines of his panorama of contemporary life; details of which could be reserved for less remote and better informed correspondents.

Much as he might protest that he was infinitely distressed that Lady Ossory showed his 'idle notes, which I cannot conceive can amuse anybody', there can be little doubt that he intended a large part of his correspondence for posthumous publication (retrieving letters for annotation when possible, copying them and destroying the originals), and here he was probably influenced by the example of Mme. de Sévigné whose letters had already become classics. Mentioning his own letters to Mann he remarked, 'then you have undone yourself with me for you compare them to Madame de Sévigné's; absolute treason! Do you know there is scarce a book in the world I love so much as her letters?' In fact, Mme. de Sévigné is the only letter writer, other than Voltaire, with whom one might compare Walpole, as she was practically the only one from whom he might have learned. Both are lively, vivid, witty and apparently spontaneous, and if Walpole never touched her highest peaks, could never strike a poetic phrase to put beside her description of the nightingale, and rarely disclosed any violent emotions, he had many qualities denied to her. In his worst fit of gout he never indulged in self-pity, he had wider interests which enabled him to sketch a larger canvas; and, what is more, he was without 'that eternal daughter of hers'.

Far from embarrassing us by endearments or boring us by subjective musings, Walpole may, perhaps, be criticized for being too reticent, since he seldom refers to himself other than in the amused self-depreciatory tone that good manners dictated. The price paid for unfailing gaiety and urbanity is inevitably a want of depth, but the compensations are so considerable that it would be as ungracious to complain of this defect in Walpole as it would be obtuse to look for

the social graces in William Cowper's letters. One of
Walpole's more questionable adages asserts that 'this world
is a comedy to those that think, a tragedy to those that feel';
and if he generally chose the comedy we need not assume
that he wanted feeling. He displayed a keen and genuine
concern for the Misses Berry on their travels; he could rise
in anger at the execution of Admiral Byng, and his deep
filial affection is unmistakable whenever he mentions his
revered father, most notably, perhaps, when he wrote on
his last visit to Houghton in 1761:

> Here I am, probably for the last time of my life, though not for
> the last time: every clock that strikes tells me I am an hour nearer
> to yonder church—that church, into which I have not yet had
> courage to enter, where lies that mother on whom I doated and who
> doated on me! There are the two rival mistresses of Houghton, neither
> of whom ever wished to enjoy it! There too lies he who founded its
> greatness, to contribute to whose fall Europe was embroiled; there
> he sleeps in quiet and dignity, while his friend and his foe, rather his
> false ally and real enemy, Newcastle and Bath, are exhausting the
> dregs of their pitiful lives in squabbles and pamphlets.

But his moments of seriousness, like his anger, his wit, his
gossip, his occasional improprieties (which squeamish Vic-
torian editors excised) or his flirtatiousness were never such
as would be inadmissible in a well conducted *salon*.

It was from a vantage point in the drawing-room that
Walpole watched the richly dressed masquerade of the
eighteenth century breathlessly dancing to its close as the
storm clouds gathered outside. He affords us no glimpse of
the low life of Fielding's London, the dapper bourgeoisie
of Richardson's provincial town or the port-stained intellectual world of The Club; nor yet does he present us at court
to waste our time in Hanoverian formalities. On one occasion he takes us to a prison, but we go with the Quality,
and in such force that the poor malefactor swoons from the
heat in his cell. Walpole's world was that of the gay, emancipated, intelligent Whig aristocracy whose civilized distinc-
tion he reflected.

Nothing (wrote Thackeray) can be more charming than Horace's letters. Fiddles sing all through them: wax-lights, fine dresses, fine jokes, fine plate, fine equippages, glitter and sparkle there: never was such a brilliant, jigging, smirking Vanity Fair as that through which he leads us.

To paint this picture of contemporary life Walpole employed an apparently free and spontaneous style which dances along on tip-toe, now echoing the measure of the minuet, now breaking into a brisk country dance and then slackening to the stately rhythm of the saraband. Never pedestrian, never pompous, his letters have a sparkling freshness which is the first of their many attractions. They appear spontaneous, but such an 'extemporary' air can be achieved only by recourse to art. 'Did you hear that scream?' he begins a letter recounting the antics of the Duchess of Kingston when apprehended for bigamy, and he contrives to turn a tedious and squalid scandal into an amusing fantasy. 'Lord, I had almost forgot', he remarks and thereby underlines a point that might escape attention. 'But how I run on', he exclaims as he brings a meandering description to an abrupt close. One of the greatest merits of Walpole's letters is that they are always kept within the bounds of their medium and never read like fragments of travel books or excerpts from histories, although containing many descriptions of places visited and of historical events.

Even when indulging in his rare 'set pieces', Walpole always managed to preserve the form of a private letter sent to a friend, though we may sometimes feel that he has allowed his eye a glance towards posterity. Consider, for instance, his account of the trial of the rebel peers after the Jacobite rising of 1745. His day to day reports of the trial show that he quickly recognized how admirably Lord Balmerino fitted the role of tragic hero,

—he is the most natural brave old fellow I ever saw: the highest intrepidity even to indifference. At the bar he behaved like a soldier and a man; in the intervals of form with carelessness and humour. He pressed extremely to have his wife, his pretty Peggy, with him in the Tower.

Lady Townshend felt differently, he tells us, and developed a passion for Lord Kilmarnock, 'smitten by his falling shoulders . . . (she) forswears conversing with the bloody English and has taken a French master'. The climax came with the execution of Balmerino:

> Then came old Balmerino, treading with the air of a general. As soon as he mounted the scaffold he read the inscription on his coffin, as he did again afterwards: he then surveyed the spectators, who were in amazing numbers, even upon masts of ships in the river; and pulling out his spectacles read a treasonable speech, which he delivered to the Sheriff, and said, the young Pretender was so sweet a Prince, that flesh and blood could not resist following him; and lying down to try the block, he said, 'If I had a thousand lives I would lay them all down here in the same cause'. He said, if he had not taken the sacrament the day before, he would have knocked down Williamson, the lieutenant of the Tower, for his ill usage of him. He took the axe and felt it, and asked the headsman how many blows he had given Lord Kilmarnock; and gave him three guineas. Two clergymen, who attended him, coming up, he said, 'No, gentleman, I believe you have already done me all the service you can'. Then he went to the corner of the scaffold, and called very loud for the warder, to give him his perriwig, which he took off, and put on a night-cap of Scotch plaid, and then pulled off his coat and waistcoat and lay down; but being told he was on the wrong side, vaulted round, and immediately gave the sign by tossing up his arm, as if he were giving the signal for battle. He received three blows, but the first certainly took away all sensation. He was not a quarter of an hour on the scaffold; Lord Kilmarnock above half a one. Balmerino certainly died with the intrepidity of a hero, but with the insensibility of one too. As he walked from his prison to execution, seeing every window and top of house filled with spectators, he cried out, 'Look, look, how they are all piled up like rotten oranges!'

It is hard to believe that so keenly observed a description could be written by one too fastidious to attend the barbarous spectacle; yet Walpole was not there, and probably relied upon an eye-witness report from the necrophilic George Selwyn. By the selection of telling details, and the superbly controlled rhythm of the prose, he presented an unforgettable account of the execution which could never form part of a formal history though it must be quoted by every conscientious historian.

In another justly celebrated passage Walpole described the funeral of George II:

> Do you know, I had the curiosity to go to the burying t'other night; I had never seen a royal funeral; nay I walked as a rag of quality, which I found would be, and so it was, the easiest way of seeing it. It is absolutely a noble sight. The Prince's chamber, hung with purple, with a quantity of silver lamps, the coffin under a canopy of purple velvet, and six vast chandeliers of silver on high stands, had a very good effect. The Ambassador from Tripoli and his son were carried to see that chamber. The procession, through a line of foot guards, every seventh man bearing a torch, the horse-guards lining the outside, their officers with drawn sabres and crape sashes on horseback, the drums muffled, the fifes, bells tolling, and minute guns,—all this was very solemn. But the charm was the entrance of the Abbey, where we were received by the Dean and Chapter in rich robes, the choir and almsmen bearing torches; the whole Abbey so illuminated, that one saw it to greater advantage than by day; the tombs, long aisles, and fretted roof, all appearing distinctly, and with the happiest *chiaro scuro*. There wanted nothing but incense, and little chapels here and there, with priests saying mass for the repose of the defunct; yet one could not complain of its not being catholic enough. I had been in dread of being coupled with some boy of ten years old; but the heralds were not very accurate, and I walked with George Grenville, taller and older, to keep me in countenance. When we came to the chapel of Henry the Seventh, all solemnity and decorum ceased; no order was observed, people sat or stood where they could or would; the yeoman of the guard were crying out for help, oppressed by the immense weight of the coffin; the Bishop read sadly, and blundered in the prayers; the fine chapter, *Man that is born of a woman*, was chanted, not read; and the anthem besides being immeasurably tedious, would have served as well for a nuptial. The real serious part was the figure of the Duke of Cumberland, heightened by a thousand melancholy circumstances. He had a dark brown adonis, and a cloak of black cloth, with a train of five yards. Attending the funeral of a father could not be pleasant:

his leg extremely bad, yet forced to stand upon it near two hours; his face bloated and distorted with his late paralytic stroke, which has affected, too, one of his eyes, and placed over the mouth of the vault, into which, in all probability, he must himself so soon descend; think how unpleasant a situation! He bore it all with a firm and unaffected countenance. This grave scene was fully contrasted by the burlesque Duke of Newcastle. He fell into a fit of crying the moment he came into the chapel, and flung himself back in a stall, the Archbishop hovering over him with a smelling bottle; but in two minutes his curiosity got the better of his hypocrisy, and he ran about the chapel with his glass to spy out who was or was not there, spying with one hand, and mopping his eyes with the other. Then returned the fear of catching cold; and the Duke of Cumberland, who was sinking with heat, felt himself weighed down, and turning round, found it was the Duke of Newcastle standing upon his train, to avoid the chill of the marble. It was very theatric to look down into the vault, where the coffin lay, attended by mourners with lights.

This is as long an account as he gives of any single occasion and one of the most masterly pieces of reportage in the language. Of course, it is artfully constructed, its spontaneity is affected and the contrast between solemnity and farce is most carefully contrived—hence its perennial freshness and brilliance.

Set pieces such as the two quoted form but a small part of Walpole's correspondence; the bulk is taken up with political news and the minor incidents of the day—marriages, intrigues and divorces, masquerades, dinner parties and routs. We are allowed to follow the *Gunningiad*, the matrimonial careers of the beautiful Misses Gunning who first took the town by storm in 1751, or of Lady Craven who lived apart from her husband for many years until she 'received the news of her Lord's death on a Friday, went into weeds on Saturday, and into white satin and many diamonds, on Sunday, and in that vestal trim was married to the Margrave of Anspach'. These lively *contes* trip gaily through scores of letters, for Walpole could always find space to record a social mishap. Yet in all his tittle-tattle there is little malice and never a word of social criticism, for he found his contemporaries absurd rather than wicked. He records the latest *bon mot* of George Selwyn, the most recent folly of the regnant beauty, the current nine day's wonder, faithfully and dispassionately to fill in the corners of his great picture of eighteenth-century life.

VI
THE DANCING SENATOR

Though always agog for the latest scandal, Walpole was much more than a gossip writer, and the ability he showed for the portrayal of society he could no less effectively apply to the political world whose intricacies he was uniquely qualified by birth and upbringing to understand from within. His own parliamentary career of twenty-six years, which began when he was 'elected' to represent a rotten borough in 1741, just as his father's long ministry was drawing to its close, was not, indeed, a particularly distinguished one. The son of an eminent father seldom avoids invidious comparison if he attempts to follow in his father's footsteps, and Horace Walpole therefore adopted a somewhat supercilious attitude towards politics; though we need not take him at this word when he wrote:

> In short, the true definition of me is that I am a dancing senator—not that I do dance, or do anything by being a senator; but I go to balls and to the House of Commons—to look on: and you will believe when I tell you that I really think the former the more serious occupation of the two: at least the performers are more in earnest.

For if he seldom spoke in the House, he could bestir himself into action behind the scenes to promote a cause which aroused his deeper feelings—to defend his father's reputation, to save Admiral Byng from the firing squad, or to jockey his cousin, hero and dearest friend, Henry Conway, into office. Having achieved his aim he would quietly withdraw and resume his role as spectator, but his experience of backstage intrigue quickened his understanding of politics and enabled him to become not only the wittiest but the acutest observer of the Parliamentary scene.

The Duke of Grafton, referring to the time when he took office as the first Lord of the Treasury in 1767, declared, 'there was no one from whom I received so just account of the various factions . . . than from Mr. Walpole . . . no person had so good means of getting to the knowledge of what was passing as himself': and historians have been equally indebted to Walpole's political observations in his letters and memoirs. In an age unchronicled by official parliamentary reports, when most crucial decisions were reached behind the scenes rather than in the debating chambers, and politics were a personal, indeed largely a family affair, the value of a commentator who could give a 'just account of the various factions' need not be emphasized. Walpole's clarity and concision of expression is hardly less remarkable than his insight; when he had set forth the ministerial changes of 1746 in a letter to Mann, he could remark with justifiable satisfaction, 'there, who would think that I had written you an entire history in the compass of three sides of paper'.

But despite his gifts and opportunities, Walpole's political comments are often marred by his weakness for jumping to conclusions. As Mr. Romney Sedgwick has remarked, 'his facts are first class and his generalizations worthless', though since his facts can so easily be separated from the rest, his value to the political historian is scarcely affected. A more serious defect arose from his belief that history, like nature, could be improved by art—a belief that led him into several misconceptions, for he could rarely resist the temptation to make a good story by putting two closely related but independent facts together. These weaknesses are evident in his highly coloured account of George III's plot to seize absolute power under the baneful influence of his mother, who was carrying on an amorous intrigue with the Prime Minister, Lord Bute. This, as Sir Lewis Namier has shown, 'was one of Walpole's "Gothic fancies", a tale rendered

mysterious and sinister by his imagination, a pattern uncon-
sciously derived from his own young years, which he
stamped upon a historical canvas'.

Throughout his life Walpole was a staunch Whig, and
there is no reason to doubt the sincerity of the liberal
opinions which give a zestful bias to his political comments.
His integrity, his perspicuity and the high moral standards
implied in his sarcasms were recognized by so unlikely an
admirer as Thomas Carlyle who considered him

> One of the clearest sighted men of the Eighteenth Century . . . a
> determined despiser and merciless dissector of cant; a liberal withal,
> one who will go to all lengths for the 'glorious revolution', and
> resist Tory principles to the death: he writes with an indignant ele-
> giac feeling, how Mr. This, who had voted so and then voted so, and
> was the son of this and the brother of that, and had such claims to the
> fat appointment, was nevertheless scandalously postponed to Mr.
> That;—whereupon are not the affairs of the nation in a bad way?

He had, indeed, few illusions about the petty wranglings,
the jobbery and charlatanism of the political world in
which his lot was cast as an observer; but he was not the
man to reform a corrupt system. 'For take notice', he told
Conway, who had just suffered a major reverse in his career,

> I do not design to fall on my own dagger, in the hopes that some
> Mr. Addison a thousand years hence may write a dull tragedy about
> me. I will write my own story a little more cheerfully than he would.

Write it he did, though not without an occasional bitter
reflection on contemporary events. Referring to the short-
sighted policy of the war against the American colonials he
asked,

> What should we gain by triumph itself? Would America laid
> waste, deluged with blood, plundered, enslaved, replace America
> flourishing, rich and free? Do we want to reign over it, as the
> Spaniards over Peru, depopulated? Are desolate regions preferable
> to commercial cities? But if the Provincials conquer, are they, like
> lovers, to kiss and be friends?

The surprisingly advanced and emancipated attitude adopted
in these remarks reveals that in politics, as in other fields,
Walpole held firm convictions. If he declined to treat politics
solemnly, he did not fail to consider them seriously.

VII
THE CONSTANT PREOCCUPATION
OF REAL AFFECTION

The reader of Walpole's letters must often find himself
wondering if their author, so abundantly endowed with
every prudent, every pleasing part, did not lack something,
and usually concludes that he wanted a heart. Inevitably,
the letters of so highly sociable a man present a social face,
but his reticence is so politely good-humoured that he seems
to tempt us to peer through his mask in search of some
passion hidden from society. His gift for friendship is mani-
fest in the variety of his attachments, for he was devoted to
such incongruous figures as the retiring, bookish Thomas Gray
and the witty, worldly George Selwyn; the pious Hannah
More—his 'most holy Hannah'—and the feckless Richard
Bentley (son of the great Master of Trinity); the exquisite
and effeminate Chute and the dull but manly Conway. And
if he was not quite the 'boundless friend and bitter but
placable enemy' he imagined himself to be, there is ample evi-
dence of his generosity with time and money to his protégées
and others in need.[1] His letters do not show a lack of warmth
so much as an equality of warmth diffused over all his

---

[1] Walpole has so unjustly been criticized for his treatment of Thomas
Chatterton that his conduct must, once again, be defended by a brief recital
of the facts. In March 1768 Chatterton, then aged sixteen, sent Walpole
what purported to be the transcript of a manuscript he had found, *The Ryse
of Peyncteynge yn Englande, wroten bie T. Rowlie, 1469, for Mastre Canynge.*
He received this document with uncritical enthusiasm and wrote a cour-
teous letter to Chatterton who then sent him some poems of his own com-
position for which he also claimed a fifteenth-century date. Although he
was struck by these verses, Walpole realized, after consultation with Gray
and Mason, that they were forgeries and he told Chatterton as much in an
avuncular letter. Chatterton committed suicide some eighteen months later.

acquaintance, for until his last years he seems to have regarded them all in the same amused, indulgent though slightly detached manner, as if forcing his emotions to obey a Stoic rule. He never allows us to see how deep his affections went, and even took care to erase most of the boyish endearments from Gray's early letters to him. But Mary Berry, who had a better right to speak on this matter than anyone else, declared:

> The affections of his heart were bestowed on few; for in early life they had never been cultivated, but they were singularly warm, pure and constant; characterized not by the ardour of passion but by the constant preoccupation of real affection.

After his mildly flirtatious *cicisbeatura* to the Marchesa Grifoni while in Florence on the Grand Tour at the age of twenty-two, he seems to have avoided any amorous entanglement, neither soliciting nor enduring the pangs of physical love. Then, in middle age, he allowed himself to be introduced into the Parisian salon of Mme. du Deffand, little suspecting the scalding passions his frail valetudinarian form might arouse in this 'blind old *débauchée* of wit'. She was sixty-nine, Walpole was delighted to discover, and had innumerable stories of court scandals of the *Régence* when, for a giddy fortnight, she had been mistress to the Regent himself. To the admirer of Mme. de Sévigné, the lively gossip, flashing repartee and formal atmosphere of the Du Deffand coterie could not fail to be entrancing. She reciprocated the attraction, charmed no doubt by his wit, his ingratiating attentions and, perhaps, his voice; but as the weeks passed she discovered that the fascinating Englishman had invaded her heart. Unaware of the intensity of passion he had awakened, Walpole continued to dance attendance upon her and was delighted to find how effortlessly he had tottered into vogue in Paris.

Middle-aged *beau* to a hardened old *salonnière* was not a role in which Walpole could see himself with any relish, and when he became aware, shortly before leaving Paris,

of the embarrassing situation into which he had stumbled,
he took fright and commanded Mme. du Deffand never to
use the word *amour* in writing to him. Terrified of ridicule,
he became increasingly alarmed at the spate of letters she
poured forth with ever mounting tenderness, until he
sharply rebuked her with indifference to his wishes. The
chilly note struck by this rebuke reveals the least amiable
aspect of Walpole's character, for his attitude to Mme. du
Deffand was governed by his dread of ridicule. To this
selfish concern he would make no concessions, though in
other ways he could be generous to his infatuated admirer.
Over a period of fifteen years, they wrote to each other
frequently, and Walpole visited her from time to time. She
wrote to him of the Paris tittle-tattle and the books that
were read to her and bored her; in his few surviving replies
he sent her news of London with suggestions for reading.
Occasionally he was so unwise as to tell her of his health,
but his mildest fit of gout was sufficient to unleash a torrent
of compassion which provoked him to another unfeeling
rebuke. He did not trouble to visit her in her last illness, and
she died knowing how little her love was requited. She left
him her papers and her lap-dog, Tonton, who was to be
seen waddling about the galleries of Strawberry for many
a year.

    Before Tonton died, Walpole became involved in an
affair of the heart which patriotic French critics have inter-
preted as a just revenge for his treatment of Mme. du
Deffand. In 1787, when he was seventy, he met Agnes and
Mary Berry, two young sisters, as handsome as they were
intelligent and refined, who soon became his closest friends.
They appreciated his collection of *virtù* and helped to add to
it; they listened enraptured to his anecdotes. For them he
wrote his *Reminiscences of the Reign of George II*, declaring,
'O Guiccardin, is posthumous renown so valuable as the
satisfaction of reading these court tales to the lovely Berrys'.
Both sisters were equally attentive to him, but much as they
protested that they were his twin wives, 'my wife Leah and

my wife Rachel', he developed for the more vivacious and
intellectual Mary a marked preference that may have been
akin to love. When they travelled round England, he pursued
them with letters advising them where to go and what to
see, letters which renewed for him the joys he had derived
from similar jaunts in his youth. But when they announced
their intention of spending the winter of 1790 abroad he was
mortified. He coaxed, he cajoled, he remonstrated without
avail; and yet worse was to come, for they planned to return
through France which was already seething with the ferment
of the Revolution. At this intelligence his consternation
knew no bounds, he poured forth a torrent of anxious heart-
felt letters to them and, casting discretion to the winds,
buttonholed everyone he met to tell of the Berrys and the
peril of their journey.

The spectacle of a septuagenarian being kittenish is seldom
attractive or edifying, yet Walpole's wry humour is so
endearing that the letters he addressed to the Berrys are
among the most charming he ever wrote. He had mellowed
without softening and even in his caducity he retained his
sharpness of eye and sprightliness of wit. Moreover, he who
had, perhaps too easily, taken all for granted, began at last
to appreciate the kindly providence which had always
watched over him and had now provided two companions
to cheer his decline. Naturally, the relationship drew upon
him the ridicule he had so long dreaded, and the town
buzzed with rumours of his imminent marriage; but he was
too old or too wise to care. Far from revenging his callousness
towards Mme. du Deffand, Mary and Agnes Berry pro-
tected him from the bitterness of age, bringing to his last
years the glow of an Indian summer, and he enjoyed their
almost constant companionship until his death in 1797.

VIII
CONCLUSION

When the first sample of Walpole's correspondence was published in 1798, Joseph Farington noted in his diary, 'the opinion of Lord Orford's letters is that they will raise his reputation as an author; that though sometimes on trifling subjects, yet never dull'. With the publication of larger and increasingly elaborate editions in the subsequent hundred and fifty years, his reputation has grown steadily, and he is now recognized as one of the greatest, if not the greatest, of all letter writers. Nevertheless, it would be misleading to regard him simply as an author of elegant and entertaining epistles. His correspondence forms but a part, albeit the largest and most important part, of a remarkable achievement in a variety of literary forms. To this versatility is due much of his power as a letter writer, for the merit of Walpole's correspondence rests on its cumulative effect rather than on the formal perfection of individual letters. Indeed, its value is inseparable from its great bulk and wide scope. Like Tolstoi and Proust in their novels and André Gide in his journals, Walpole required the grand scale and achieved his finest effects by a slow and patient process of accumulation.

For rather more than half a century he recorded the day to day preoccupations of the society in which he lived, and his letters present a unique picture of England in this period. Some elements seem, in the light of other accounts, to be a little distorted; some are omitted altogether, but the picture as a whole is an authentic representation of the social and political scene as it struck a contemporary. Other writers have described the appearance and actions of Lord Bute, Charles James Fox, George Selwyn and Lady Mary Wortley Montagu, but Walpole alone tells us what it was like to live among them. Not content with recording the progress of the 1745 rebellion or the French Revolution, he vividly describes how it felt to wait in London as the Pretender's army marched southwards or to receive the first intelligence of the horrors committed in France. Of course, such immediacy of impression could only be obtained at the expense of coherency and a general historical pattern, but Walpole was always more interested in the effect great events had on himself and his friends than in the events themselves. He was, in a sense, our first social historian, even though he limited his attention to a relatively small section of the community.

At first blush, the creator of Strawberry Hill and the author of *The Castle of Otranto* may appear an eccentric, but on closer inspection he is found to share nearly all the prejudices, aspirations and civilized pleasures of the emancipated upper-class society of which he was so notable a member. His attitude to Gothic architecture, history, the landscape, the Sensibility Cult and to life in all its joys and sorrows, as revealed in his letters and books, is entirely characteristic of his time and class. The picture of eighteenth-century England which emerges from his work is consequently drawn with as much sympathy as brilliance. For it is also the expression of a fascinating human personality; a self-portrait which reveals selfishness, pettiness and frivolity as well as affection, humour and seriousness, suggesting a lonely melancholy beneath the glitter of the surface. Horace Walpole was not only the gay social charmer—'spirits of hartshorn' as Lady Townshend called him—but the persevering scholar and shy recluse who sheltered behind a series of social masks. In his works, as on some great rococo ceiling, we are allowed to see the author's slender form mingling with the crowd of figures; now peering out from a group of dancing masqueraders, now accompanying a file of pompous senators or reclining at his ease and complacently watching the rich pageant of his own creation.

HORACE WALPOLE

A Select Bibliography

(Place of publication London unless stated otherwise)

Bibliographies:

THE BIBLIOGRAPHY OF THE STRAWBERRY HILL PRESS, by A. T. Hazen. Yale (1942).

A BIBLIOGRAPHY OF HORACE WALPOLE, by A. T. Hazen. Yale (1948).

HORACE WALPOLE'S LIBRARY, by W. S. Lewis (1957).
The Sandars Lectures at Cambridge, 1957.

Note: The library (Bibliotheca Arbuteana) of Wilmarth Sheldon Lewis at Farmington, Conn., contains an incomparable collection of printed books, MSS., autographs, memorabilia, etc., by, or relating to, Walpole.

Collected Works:

FUGITIVE PIECES IN VERSE AND PROSE, 2 vols. Strawberry Hill (1770).

THE WORKS OF HORATIO WALPOLE, EARL OF ORFORD, 5 vols. (1798).
The nominal editor of these volumes was Robert Berry, but his daughter, Mary Berry, seems to have done all the editorial work. Additional volumes pendant to these were published later: *Letters . . . to George Montagu* and *Letters . . . to the Rev. William Cole* (often bound in one volume) (1818), *Memoires . . . of George II*, 2 vols. (1822), *Letters . . . to the Earl of Hertford*, etc. (1825). See below.

Separate Works:

THE LESSONS FOR THE DAY (1742). *Political pamphlet.*

THE BEAUTIES. AN EPISTLE TO MR. ECKARDT, THE PAINTER (1746). *Verse.*
A corrected version appeared in *Dodsley's Collection of Poems*, 1748.

EPILOGUE TO TAMERLANE (1746). *Verse.*
This *Epilogue* to Rowe's *Tamerlane* was spoken by Mrs. Pritchard at Covent Garden Theatre on 4 and 5 November 1746.

AEDES WALPOLIANAE: OR, A DESCRIPTION OF THE COLLECTION OF PICTURES AT HOUGHTON HALL IN NORFOLK (1747). *Catalogue* (of Sir Robert Walpole's collection).

A LETTER TO THE WHIGS (1747). *Political pamphlet.*

A SECOND AND THIRD LETTER TO THE WHIGS (1748). *Political pamphlet.*

THE ORIGINAL SPEECH OF SIR WILLIAM STANHOPE (1748). *Political pamphlet.*

THE SPEECH OF RICHARD WHITELIVER (1748). *Political pamphlet.*

A LETTER FROM XO HO, A CHINESE PHILOSOPHER AT LONDON, TO HIS FRIEND LIEN CHI AT PEKING (1757). *Political pamphlet.*
An attack on the political situation through the mouth of an imaginary Chinaman.

A CATALOGUE OF ROYAL AND NOBLE AUTHORS, 2 vols. (1758). *Bio-bibliography.*
A *Postscript* was printed at Strawberry Hill in 1786.

FUGITIVE PIECES IN VERSE AND PROSE. Strawberry Hill (1758).
Horace Walpole's first collection of his verses, with a few essays.

A DIALOGUE BETWEEN TWO GREAT LADIES (1760). *Political Satire.*
A brief satire on the German war.

A CATALOGUE OF THE PICTURES AND DRAWINGS IN THE HOLBEIN CHAMBER (1760).
Walpole's first catalogue of his own collection.

ANECDOTES OF PAINTING IN ENGLAND, 5 vols. Strawberry Hill (1762–71). *Bio-iconography.*

THE OPPOSITION TO THE LATE MINISTER VINDICATED (1763). *Political pamphlet.*

THE MAGPIE AND HER BROOD, A FABLE: ADDRESSED TO MISS HOTHAM. Strawberry Hill (1764).

A COUNTER-ADDRESS TO THE PUBLIC, ON THE LATE DISMISSION OF A GENERAL OFFICER (1764). *Political pamphlet.*
A reply to a pamphlet attacking Walpole's cousin, General H. S. Conway.

THE CASTLE OF OTRANTO (1765). *Novel.*

AN ACCOUNT OF THE GIANTS LATELY DISCOVERED (1766).
A satirical letter on the state of England.

HISTORIC DOUBTS ON THE LIFE AND REIGN OF KING RICHARD III (1768). *History.*

THE MYSTERIOUS MOTHER. Strawberry Hill (1768). *Drama.*

A REPLY TO THE OBSERVATIONS OF THE REV. DR. MILLES, ON THE WARD ROBE ACCOUNT. Strawberry Hill (1770).
A reply to Dr. Milles's criticism of *Historic Doubts*.

A DESCRIPTION OF STRAWBERRY HILL. Strawberry Hill (1774). *Catalogue.*

A LETTER TO THE EDITORS OF THE MISCELLANIES OF THOMAS CHATTERTON. Strawberry Hill (1779).
Walpole's defence of his conduct.

AN ESSAY ON MODERN GARDENING. Strawberry Hill (1785).
Reprinted from the Volume 4 of the *Anecdotes of Painting*.

HIEROGLYPHIC TALES. Strawberry Hill (1785). *Juvenile.*
Five fantasies written for H. S. Conway's children.

NOTES TO THE PORTRAITS AT WOBURN ABBEY (1800). *Iconography.*

REMINISCENCES WRITTEN FOR MISS MARY AND MISS AGNES BERRY (1805).
Autobiography.

MEMOIRS OF THE REIGNS OF GEORGE II AND GEORGE III (1822–59). *History.*
Published in three instalments: *The Memoires of the last ten years of the Reign of King George II* (1822); *Memoirs of the Reign of King George III* (1845); and *Journal of the Reign of King George III from 1771 to 1783* (1859).

NOTES ON LORD CHESTERFIELD'S WORKS (1867). *Criticism.*

NOTES ON THE POEMS OF ALEXANDER POPE (1871). *Criticism.*

JOURNAL OF THE PRINTING OFFICE AT STRAWBERRY HILL (1923).

STRAWBERRY HILL ACCOUNTS. Edited by P. Toynbee. Oxford (1927).
These two works cover the history and management of Walpole's private press.

MISCELLANEOUS ANTIQUITIES, edited by W. S. Lewis, 14 vols. Yale (1927–40).
Fourteen volumes of works by or closely related to Walpole, including MSS. printed for the first time: *Manuscript Commonplace Book 1780–3* (1927); *Horace Walpole's Fugitive Verses* (1931); *Anecdotes told me by Lady Denbigh* (1932); *The Duchess of Portland's Museum* (1936); *Memoranda Walpoliana* (1937).

A JOURNAL OF VISITS TO COUNTRY SEATS, edited by P. Toynbee (1927–28).
Transactions of the Walpole Society, Vol. XVI.

SELECT OBSERVATIONS. New Haven, U.S.A. (1937).
Extracts from Walpole's third *Book of Materials* of 1786.

Collected Letters:

LETTERS FROM THE HON. HORACE WALPOLE TO GEORGE MONTAGU, ESQ.
FROM THE YEAR 1736, TO THE YEAR 1770, edited by J. Martin (1818).

LETTERS FROM THE HON. HORACE WALPOLE TO THE REV. WILLIAM COLE
AND OTHERS; FROM THE YEAR 1745, TO THE YEAR 1782, edited by
J. Martin (1818).

PRIVATE CORRESPONDENCE OF HORACE WALPOLE, EARL OF ORFORD. Now
first collected, 4 vols. (1820).

LETTERS FROM THE HONBLE. HORACE WALPOLE TO THE EARL OF HERTFORD,
edited by J. W. Croker (1825).

LETTERS TO SIR HORACE MANN, edited by Lord Dover, 3 vols. (1833).

THE LETTERS OF HORACE WALPOLE, EARL OF ORFORD, edited by J. Wright,
6 vols. (1840).

LETTERS TO SIR HORACE MANN, SECOND SERIES, edited by Lord Dover,
4 vols. (1843–4).

LETTERS ADDRESSED TO THE COUNTESS OF OSSORY, edited by R. V. Smith,
2 vols. (1848).

CORRESPONDENCE OF HORACE WALPOLE AND WILLIAM MASON, edited by
J. Mitford, 2 vols. (1851).

THE LETTERS OF HORACE WALPOLE, edited by P. Cunningham, 9 vols.
(1857).

SOME UNPUBLISHED LETTERS OF HORACE WALPOLE, edited by Sir S.
Walpole (1902).

THE LETTERS OF HORACE WALPOLE, edited by Mrs. P. Toynbee, 16 vols.
(1903–5).
Three supplementary volumes edited by P. Toynbee were added to
this series, 1918–25.

THE CORRESPONDENCE OF GRAY, WALPOLE, WEST AND ASHTON 1734–
1771, edited by P. Toynbee, 2 vols. (1915).

THE YALE EDITION OF HORACE WALPOLE'S CORRESPONDENCE, edited by
W. S. Lewis. Yale (1937–continuing).
This monumental work, which is in course of publication, will be
completed in some fifty volumes and will form the definitive edition

of Walpole's correspondence. It includes a large number of letters written to him. The following correspondences have been published to date: W. Cole (2 vols.); Mme du Deffand and Wiart (6 vols.); G. Montagu (2 vols.); Mary and Agnes Berry (2 vols.); Gray, West and Ashton (2 vols.); Middleton, Dalrymple, etc. (1 vol.); Chatterton, Zouch, etc. (1 vol.); Sir H. Mann (3 vols.); William Mason (2 vols.).

Selected Letters:

LETTERS OF HORACE WALPOLE, edited by C. B. Lucas (1904).

SELECT LETTERS OF HORACE WALPOLE, edited by A. D. Greenwood (1914).

LETTERS OF HORACE WALPOLE, edited by D. M. Stuart (1914).

SELECTED LETTERS OF HORACE WALPOLE, edited by W. Hadley (1926). *Everyman's Library* edition.

A SELECTION OF THE LETTERS OF HORACE WALPOLE, edited by W. S. Lewis, 2 vols. New York (1926).

LETTERS OF HORACE WALPOLE, edited by W. S. Lewis (1951).

Some Critical and Biographical Studies:

CRITICAL AND HISTORICAL ESSAYS, by T. B. Macaulay (1843). Includes the attack on Walpole which Macaulay published in *The Edinburgh Review*, October 1833.

HORACE WALPOLE AND HIS WORLD, by L. B. Seeley (1884).

HORACE WALPOLE, A MEMOIR, by A. Dobson. New York (1890).

HOURS IN A LIBRARY, by Sir L. Stephen (1909). Includes a somewhat cold appreciative essay on Horace Walpole.

HORACE WALPOLE'S WORLD, by A. D. Greenwood (1913).

HORACE WALPOLE THE GREAT LETTER WRITER, by J. H. Edge. Dublin (1913).

BOOKS AND CHARACTERS, by L. Strachey (1922). Includes a brilliant essay on Horace Walpole and Madame du Deffand.

LA VIE D'UN DILETTANTE: HORACE WALPOLE, par P. Yvon. Paris (1924). A monumental biography.

HORACE WALPOLE AS A POET, par P. Yvon. Paris (1924).

HORACE WALPOLE, by D. M. Stuart (1927).
In the *English Men of Letters* series.

THE LIFE OF HORACE WALPOLE, by S. Gwynn (1932).

CHARACTERS AND COMMENTARIES, by L. Strachey (1933).
Includes three perceptive essays on Horace Walpole.

HORACE WALPOLE AND THE ENGLISH NOVEL, by K. K. Mehrota. Oxford (1934).

HORACE WALPOLE: A BIOGRAPHY, by R.W. Ketton-Cremer (1940).
The standard life of Walpole. A revised edition was published in 1946.

COLLECTOR'S PROGRESS, by W. S. Lewis (1952).
The autobiography of W. S. Lewis, collector of Walpoliana and editor of the Yale edition of Horace Walpole's letters, contains many acute comments on Walpole.